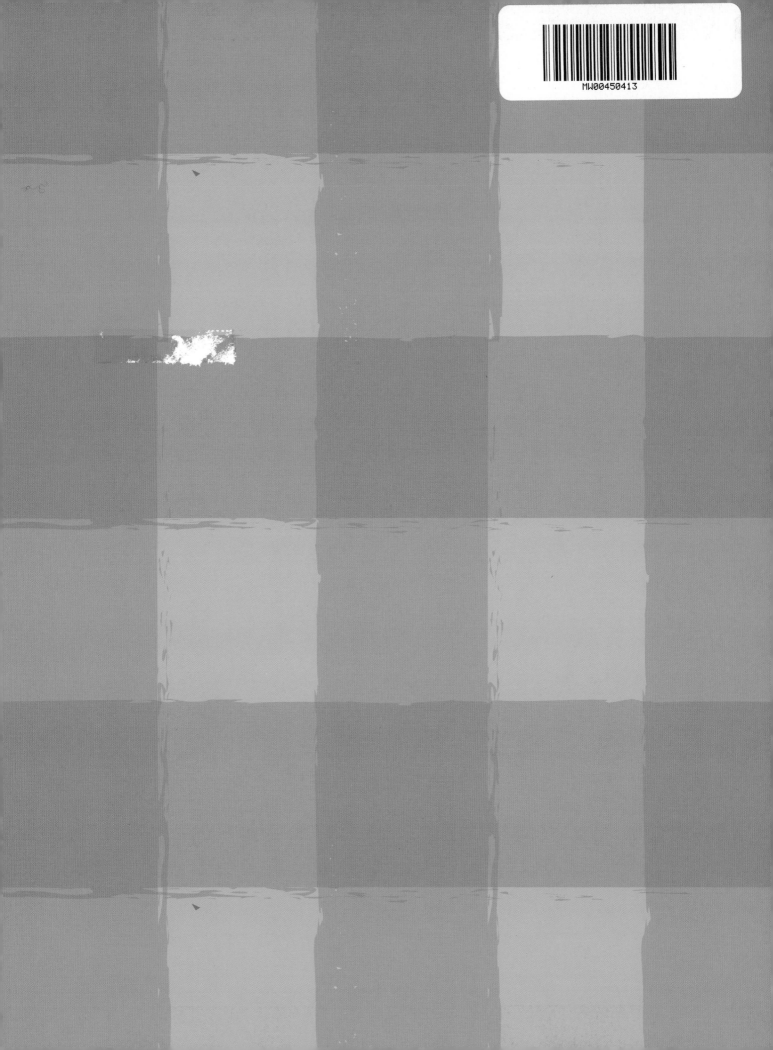

MW00450413

How Our FAMILY PRAYS Each Day

A Read-Aloud Story for Catholic Families

By Gregory K. Popcak

Illustratrated by Jacob Flores-Popcak

AVE MARIA PRESS **AVE** Notre Dame, Indiana

To all the Catholic Households on Mission.
May God bless you with his abundant love.

Founded in 1865, Ave Maria Press is a ministry of the United States Province of Holy Cross.

www.avemariapress.com

Hardcover: ISBN-13 978-1-64680-169-5

Cover and interior illustrations ©2022 Jacob Flores-Popcak.

Cover and text design by Katherine Robinson.

Printed in China.

Library of Congress Cataloging-in-Publication Data is available.

A Note for Parents

How to Use This Book

Storytime is an important family ritual. *How Our Prays Each Day* is a read-aloud book you can enjoy together as a family. Spending time with Marty's family—including their pet pelican, Pascha!—you will discover that, when families pray together, they invite God to become part of their daily lives. By bringing God with you and talking with him throughout your day, you can all get closer to God—and to one another—as you respond in prayer to the blessings and challenges you encounter along the way.

Many families feel intimidated by the idea of family prayer. We hope that *How Our Family Prays Each Day* will illustrate how simple, easy, and engaging family prayer can be. Use this book to spark important conversations about all the ways you can pray as a family. As you read together, let God show you how to discover the plan he has for the "domestic church" that is your family.

So why, you might ask, does Marty's family have a pet pelican named Pascha? The pelican is an ancient symbol of the Eucharist, and the word "Pascha" means "Easter bread." Their pet pelican is a sign that Marty's family is doing their best to bring the grace of the Eucharist home with them throughout the whole week. Just like God's grace is ever present, Pascha is always in the picture. Discuss how he is representing God's grace as you read the book together.

If you'd like more support in becoming a more joyful, peaceful, grace-filled household, please visit Catholic Households on Mission at CatholicHOM.com.

God loves our family very much,
and we all love him too.
We all try hard to ask his help
with everything we do.

Each Sunday, we all go to Mass
for special time with Jesus.
In Communion we receive the Lord.
God gives us grace to free us . . .

To love like him and give up
all our selfish ways of living.
At Mass, the Lord reminds us we
were made for love and giving.

When Mass time ends we all make sure
we don't leave God behind.
We pray, "Lord, please come home with us
and help us to be kind."

My family talks to God all week
in lots of different ways.
I'm Marty! Here's my story about
how my family prays.

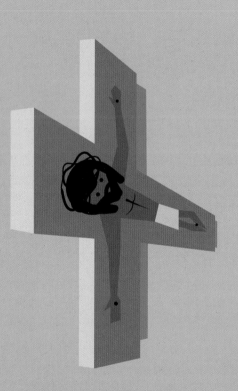

We say, "Good Morning, Jesus!"
when we wake up every day.
We ask the Lord for help
before we go
our separate ways.

We cuddle for a minute.
Then we talk a little while
and list what we could do that day
to make each other smile.

Then, when we're going out the door,
our family shares a gift;
we give each other blessings,
and it gives us all a lift.

We make a small Sign of the Cross
right on each other's heads.
We pray, "God, please take care of us
throughout the day ahead."

Of course, we bless each other in lots of other moments too. Like before the game, a test, or when we're doing something new.

And if one of us gets hurt, feels sad or scared, or has a struggle, we bless that person as we pray, "God, help them through their troubles."

When our family's running errands
or we're going out someplace,
my mom and dad say, "Look around
for small moments of grace."

When nice surprises happen,
or the day is warm and bright,
we praise God and say, "Thank you, Lord,
for making things 'just right'!"

Sometimes we see an ambulance
whiz by, or the police.
We all pray a "Hail Mary" and
ask God to give his peace.

We ask the Lord to bless everyone
who's struggling or in pain.
We pray, "God, please pour out your
love and make things right again."

Sometimes my sister makes me mad
and we argue with each other.
And I get annoyed when Mom asks,
"Can you watch your baby brother?"

But Mom and Dad are patient
and they help us put things right.
They'll say, "Let us ask the Lord for grace
to help us not to fight."

And guess what?
Somehow with God's grace
our fighting finally ends.
God helps us learn from our mistakes
and be even better friends.

Whenever we eat we all say grace
so God will bless our meal.
Then we talk about the day
and all take turns as we reveal
the highs-and-lows in each person's day.

There's joking and there's laughter.
And then?
My family—altogether—
cleans up the kitchen after.

Sometimes we're tired and cleaning's hard,
but we try to make it fun.
I think it makes God smile when
we're a team and act like one.

Usually, after dinner,
we make time for "Family Praise."
We like to try to worship God
in lots of different ways.

Some nights, we pray the Rosary,
or sing praise and worship songs.
Or Mom or Dad share Bible stories
and we all read along.

We pray for others too,
like my friend Sam who broke his arm.
We ask that God would heal their hurts
and keep them safe from harm.

If we have a special problem,
then we pray about that too.
It's good to ask for God's help when
you don't know what to do.

Our family's busy every night.
There's always lots to do.
But we all bring Jesus with us,
and he helps us
make it through ...

'Til we come back home together
and we hug each other tight.
I love my family! ("Thank you, Lord,
for making *us* 'just right.'")

At night our family gathers
one more time just before bed.
We pray for restful sleep
and peaceful dreams to fill our heads.

We ask our guardian angels
to watch over us through the night
and keep us safe until God wakes us
with his morning light.

Some people say our family prays a lot.
I guess that's true ...
But I'm glad.
Because it makes God part of
everything we do.

God helps our family be
a little closer every day.
He fills our hearts
and home with love.
That's why our family prays.

This Sunday, when your family goes to Mass, keep this in mind. Pray, "Lord Jesus, please come home with us and help us to be kind."

I know that just like God helps us,
he wants to help you too,
and fill your home with all his love.
That's MY family's prayer ...
for YOU!

Domestic Church Prayer

Lord Jesus Christ,

Transform our family into a true
domestic church.

Teach us to love and cherish each other,
just as you love and cherish us.

Connect our hearts as we work, play,
talk, and pray together.

Remind us to take care of each other
and everyone we meet.

Let our family be the blessing you
created us to be.

Holy Family, pray for us!

CATHOLIC HÔM
households on mission

Resources

How Our Family Prays Each Day is part of CatholicHŌM (Catholic Households on Mission), a ministry that helps Catholic families like yours to encounter Christ more meaningfully at home, and to experience their faith as the source of the warmth in their home.

If you'd like to discover more ways for you to become the family God is calling you to be, we invite you to visit CatholicHOM.com. Check out our animated CatholicHŌM webseries, order the CatholicHŌM Activity Kits, and meet the many families who are part of our active, online CatholicHŌM community. Let us help your family become a Catholic Household on Mission—a truly loving, joyful, grace-filled, CatholicHŌM.